101 Cognitive Errors
Decision Making

Dr. Mostafa Maleki Tehrani

© Firouz Media 2023
All rights reserved

No parts of this publication may be reproduced, stored in a retrieval system, or transmitted in any form or by any means, electronic, mechanical, photocopying, recording, or otherwise, without the prior permission of the publisher.

Firouz Media Limited
www.firouzmedia.com
IG: @firouzmedia

Digital ISBN   978-1-915557-14-8
Paperback ISBN   978-1-915557-15-5

Cover picture: Artefacti
Stock images: Pexels_Adobe_Pixabay

101 Cognitive Errors: Decision Making
Creator: Dr. Mostafa Maleki Tehrani

Preface

We can divide the decision errors into perceptual errors and logical errors.

Perceptual errors in decision-making can occur when an individual has a false understanding of their subject or environment, leading to a wrong perception. Logical errors in decision-making are errors caused by mistakes in performance, such as incorrect calculations, faulty reasoning, and incomplete information.

Accurate recognition of each error can prevent disaster in one's personal life, work, and activity. There are so many common mistakes that habitually affect the decisions we make and unconsciously lead us to a crisis.

The human mind and brain, as an organic part, sometimes suffer from errors. Still, because it comes from the decision-making center of the mind, something complicated to analyze whether this decision is correct or not, since one should give an opinion on the correctness or incorrectness of a process is where the error occurs. Therefore, accurate knowledge of various mistakes in the decision-making field helps bring the mind closer to its correct position and precise goals.

In this book, I introduced the errors briefly by presenting errors and a practical example of them. Still, it is essential to mention that these definitions can be much more diverse and broad. This classification is the product of my studies and dear and respected professors; with their help, this collection and compilation were possible. I thank every one of them.

—Mostafa Maleki Tehrani

Courtesy of Andre Fellipe

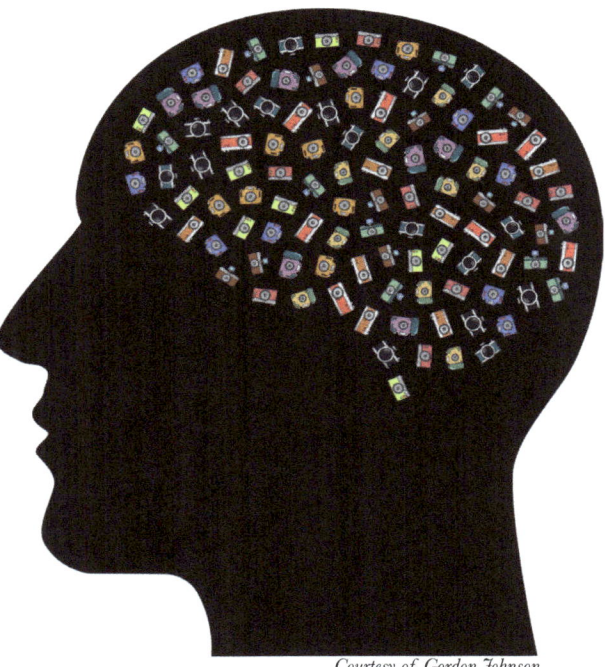

Courtesy of Gordon Johnson

1 Selective Attention Error

Our mind, unlike a camera, can only record what it focuses on.
In physics, this problem is called selective absorption and repulsion and is the major factor for the separation of color and light. This perceptual error causes the phenomenon of blindness to change.

2
Similar to Mine Error

Demonstrating interest and attention to those who have more in common with us. The same gender, the same language, the same city, etc…, and any other "same" are one of these types of mistakes.

Courtesy of Hudson Marques

Courtesy of Elliot Ogbeiwi

3

Selective Absorption Error

I ignore everything that contradicts my previous knowledge.

Courtesy of Shahbazshah91

4 Confirmation Error

Human ambition causes us to make decisions that we already know are going to be approved by others.

5 Self-Facilitation Error

The desire to take the path of least resistance is a common mistake that can lead to poor decision-making.

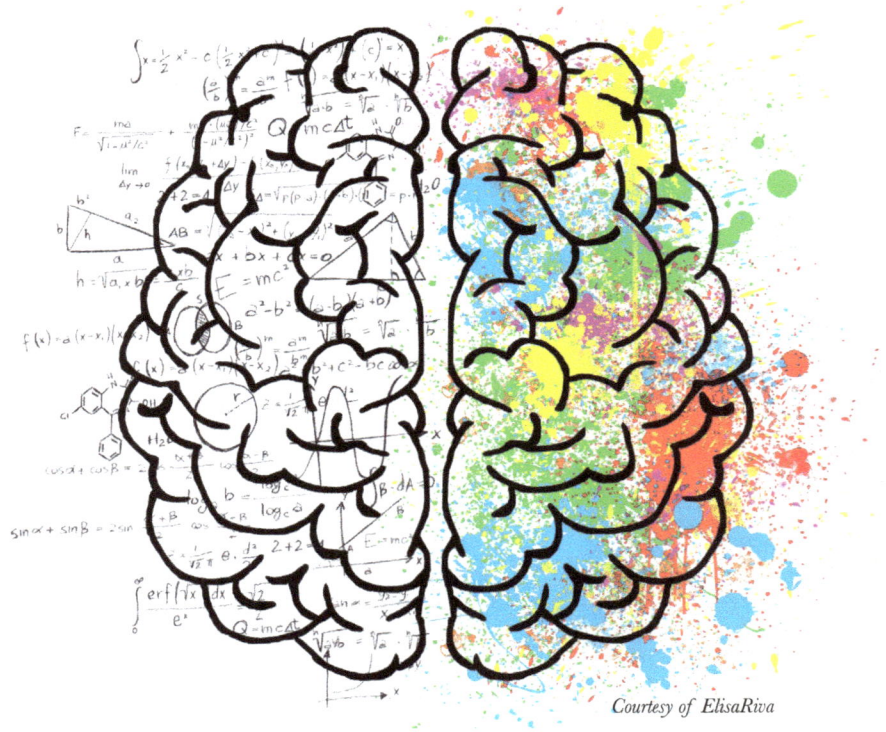

Courtesy of ElisaRiva

6 **The Basic Error of Citation** (error of psychological protection of the brain)

Everything that is good is because of our own performance, and we attribute everything that is bad to others. They gave me a low grade, or they fined me; But I got an A, or I followed the rules.

Courtesy of Sebastiaan Stam

7 Stereotype Error

When people make assumptions about others based on stereotypes, leading to incorrect judgments and decisions, making assumptions about someone else's capabilities or beliefs based on their race, gender, or other similar factors.
For instance, "Rich people are heartless."

8 Aura Error (brain indolence)

The other aspects also stand out because of a subject's significant good or bad effects. For instance, "Handsome people are smart."

9 The Error of Total

Seeing a part of the whole causes prejudgment.

For instance, "Frozen street causes slipping." However, not having proper shoes is the key factor.

Courtesy of KoolShooters

10
Pygmalion Effect Error

Humans react positively to the level of expectations of others.

"Expectation that a boxer will win."

Courtesy of Gerd Altmann

11
Justification Error

For various reasons, we minimize our own role in a wrong decision and pretend to be blameless.

"He himself teased me to react harshly."

12 The Error of Passing the Blame

One of the worst types of errors is this error that causes the loss of spirituality The most obvious example is "I am only carrying orders" When we leave the area of accountability for a wrong decision to others, even the most severe and brutal acts become humane Just by mentioning this one sentence that "responsibility for this work is not yours", they destroy the moral conscience of the society.

13 The Error of the Survivers

Incorrect sampling of the survived cases makes it impossible to find the cause of the failures. Studying the damaged planes and strengthening the vulnerable points instead of examining the crashed planes and their damaged points in the war.

Courtesy of Rémi Berger

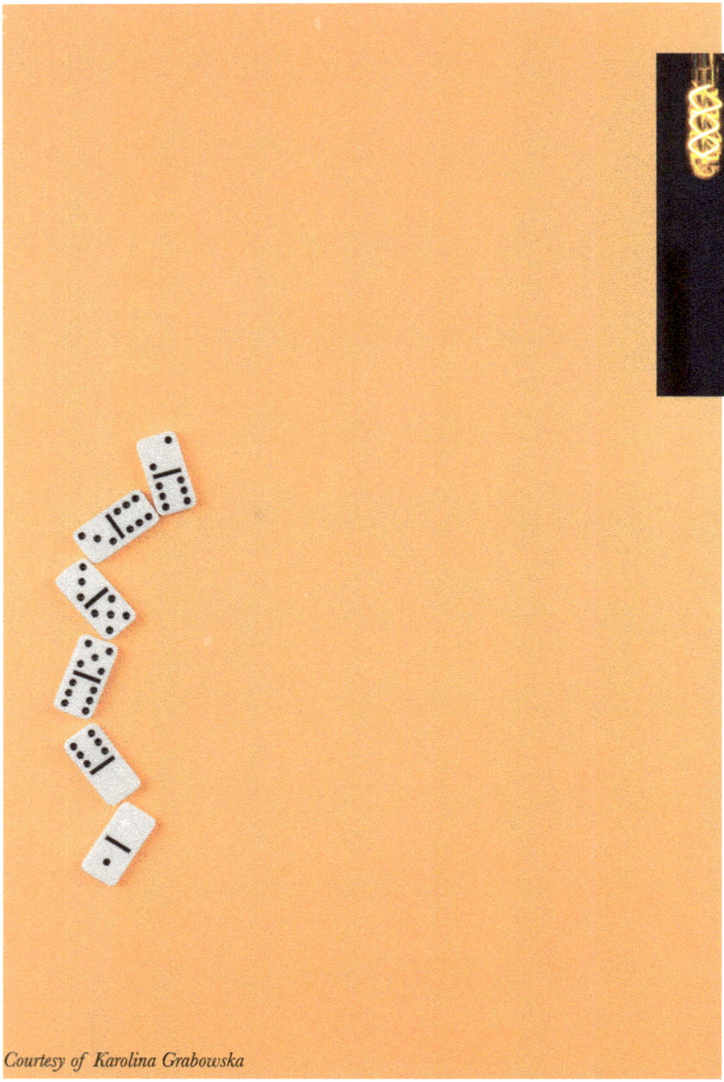

Courtesy of Karolina Grabowska

Courtesy of Juhaszmrus

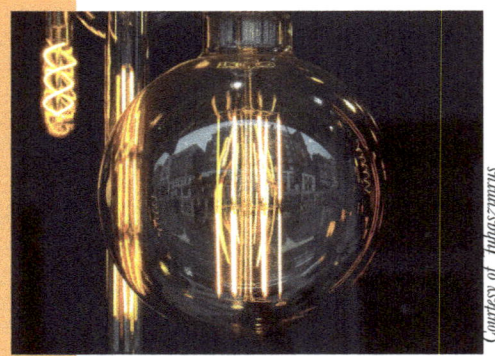

14

The Error of the Upcoming Options

It happens when we just want to take the best option from the most available basket.

Courtesy of lil artsy

15 Error of Causality and Correlation

It is not possible to conclude from two correlated variables,
one is the success factor the other.
"Every good thing is not necessarily a sign of a favorable event."

Courtesy of Stefan Stefancik

16
Flight Puzzle Error

Only having tangible tools is not the factor in success.

Does having wings and feathers alone makes flying happen? We are ignoring the role of the lifting force in flight.

Courtesy of Roman Odintsov

17 Relative and Absolute Risk Error

Lack of sound understanding of the two concepts of relative and absolute risk causes this phenomenon. When we intend to lie with statistics, we go for this type of error.
"Does the use of second-generation and third-generation seasonal antiallergic tablets double the possibility of blood clots in the lungs?"

Courtesy of Ron Lach

18
It Must Have a Reason Error

This error is one of the common errors that has become a habit among people culturally. For instance, changing the size of the Independent newspaper from large to small, after which other newspapers also did this without knowing the reason. This error creates a taboo in society.

19 The Error of Small Decisions

Instead of focusing on important issues, we spend our time and energy on less important and normal issues.

Courtesy of Juan Pablo Serrano Arenas

Courtesy of Efraim Emaki

20 Decision Viral Effect Error

Neglecting or addressing an issue can cause major incidents.
For example, ignoring safety procedures or not consulting stakeholders in long time can lead to disastrous consequences.
"Catching a cold does not occur immediately after exposure to extreme cold weather."

Courtesy of Arshdeep Singh

21
Error of Desire to Move

When our mind orders us to start a task ahead of its time.

"Jumping error of the goalkeepers."

Courtesy of Nataliya Vaitkevich

22
Average Error

Considering exponential distribution instead of Gaussian distribution when the majority of a review is all around the average.

23
Optimism Error

We should not promote optimism where people's performance does not affect the result.

"Betting on something with an uncertain outcome is an example of this."

Courtesy of Cottonbro

24 Competition Element Error

Doing undesirable thing to achieve a desirable result.
"Are you willing to kill another innocent person to save the lives of 5 innocent people?"

25 Prison Error

Creating restrictions for competitors or culprits provides the opportunity for unity between them.
Prison alone is the factor in creating unity and education and finding employment among criminals.

Courtesy of Karina Zhukovskaya

26 Balloon Error

When we press a balloon full of air, the area under pressure appears to be emptied of air, but the volume of air inside has not reduced. We should not expect to solve a problem by applying a simple solution.

"USA spraying of drug farms in South America led to farm displacement, not drug elimination."

27 The Error of Generalizing the Micro Level to the Macro Level

Micro decisions cannot be generalized to society.

"One might not allow their daughter to marry a thief, but can we ban thieves from getting married?"

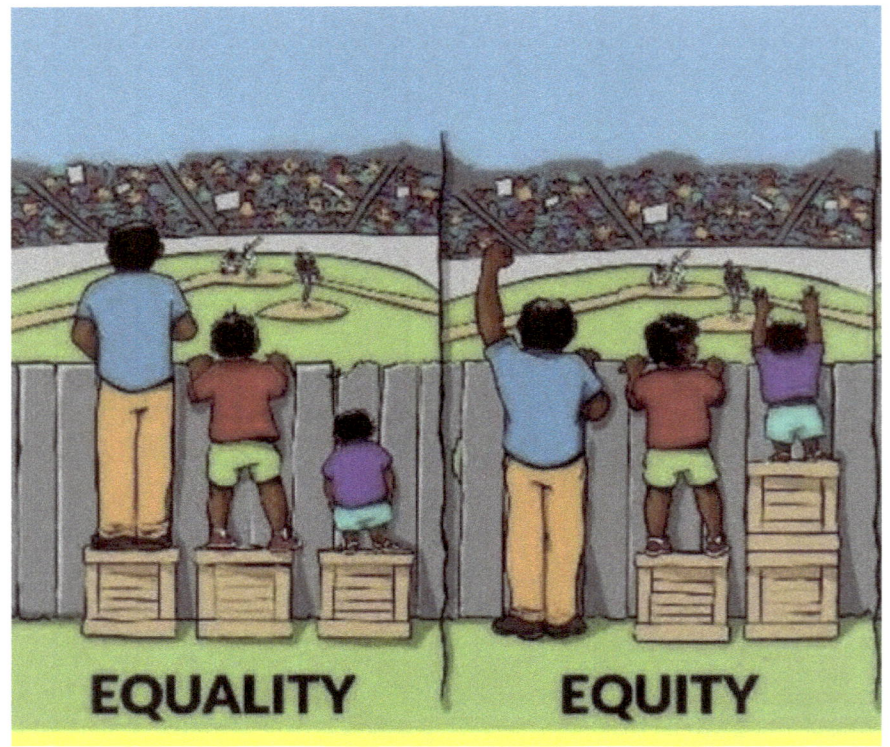

Courtesy of Interaction Institute (Social Change/Angus Maguire)

28 Error of Justice and Equality

Uniform distribution of resources does not lead to equalization of all factors.

Courtesy of Michael Burrowes

29 Measurement Error

This error occurs when the measurement tool is wrong, or it doesn't work correctly, or we don't know how to use it properly.

Courtesy of Steve Buissinne

30 Wrong Tool Error

No matter the task at hand, it is essential to use the right tools to ensure success. If a job requires precision, accuracy, and fine motor skills, a hammer is not the correct tool for the job. This idea is true for any field, from carpentry to business. When the wrong tools are used, the job at hand can become much more difficult than it needs to be.

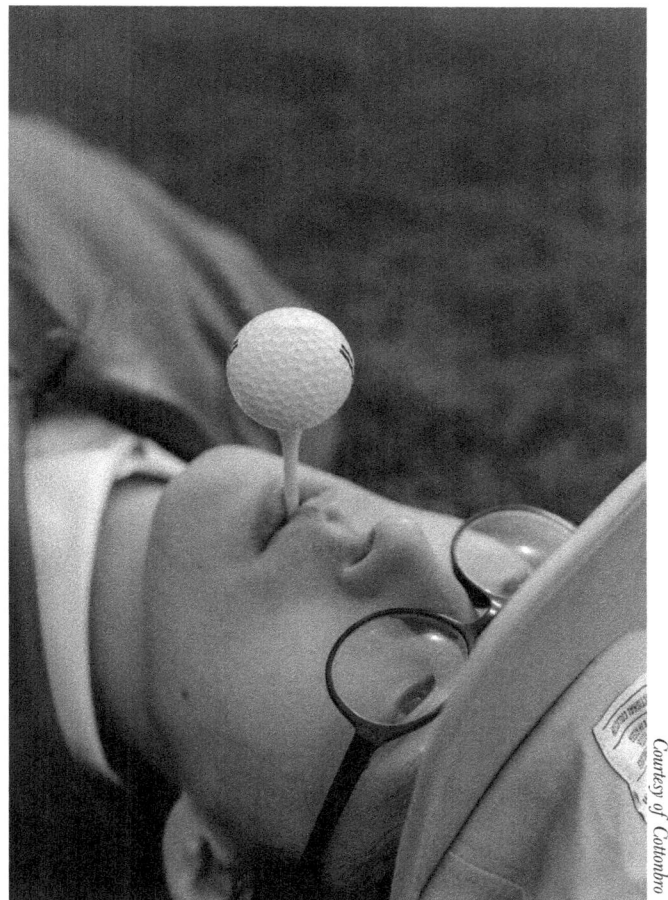

31 Inspirational Prediction Error

When our expectations and perceptions are far from reality.

"Bank failure in 1948 was not caused by economic inflation, but by depositors withdrawing their deposits based on a wrong assumption."

32 Swimmer's Body Error

Do all swimmers have a balanced body or those who have a balanced body go for swimming?

33 Projection Error

When we are not ready to accept our weaknesses and malfunctions.

"For instance, we make others look a hundred times stingier to hide our stinginess."

Courtesy of Ryan McGuire

34 The Error of Ambiguous or General thinking

Failure to separate problems into small parts made us consider the occurrence of a large phenomenon as a big factor.

Courtesy of Andrea Piacquadio

35 The Mistake of Looking Down on Others

"Eugene Carter" realized that many managers, in case of a new incident and event, try to downplay that incident and their ability to solve the problem, which has led to the failure and frustration of many.

"The rival cannot be poor and helpless."

36
Exaggerated Generalization Error

By exaggerating a problem, a person thinks it is bigger, and more important than it is.

37
Error of Supporting a Specific Solution

Maslow believed that anyone who holds a hammer sees others as nails. Therefore, when a person has only one tool in hand, he tries to see all problems in a way that can be solved with this tool.

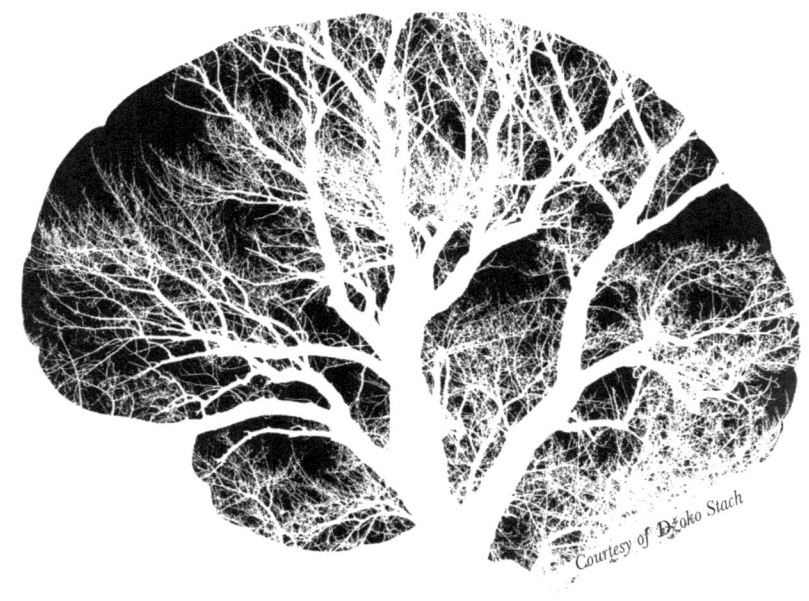

38 Error of Polarized Thinking

Having a positive or negative, black or white view on issues and not paying attention to other dimensions of an issue causes this type of perception error.

39 Failure Avoidance Error
(loss evasion)

Instead of achieving success, we only avoid failure.

Courtesy of Andrea Piacquadio

40 Memory Bias Error

Scientists know memory bias as a "heuristic error of the human brain." Memory bias says that if we remember something, it must be important or at least more important than other things that are easily remembered.

Courtesy of Anastasia Shuraeva

41
A Survivorship Orientation Error

A survivorship orientation focuses on people or things that have survived a situation, but at the same time ignores those that have not, simply because it does not see them.

"There are thousands of articles about Bill Gates and Steve Jobs dropping out of college and then going on to make legendary careers and income, but we only see a few."

Courtesy of Anna Shvets

42
Anchor Orientation Error

Determining the anchor is used in negotiations; Because the value of an offer is strongly influenced by the first suitable number or the anchor that lays the foundation of the negotiation.

Courtesy of Andrea Piacquadio

43
Origin of the Idea Orientation Error

This orientation is based on a simple theorem:
"If it hasn't occurred to me (or us), it must be worthless."

Courtesy of Matheus Bertelli

44 Error of Focusing on the latest Information

Every new piece of information is not necessarily the best and the most worthy in that field.

"When we go to the dealership after a lot of research to buy a phone, and we encounter an angry customer who is upset about the poor responsiveness of the after-sales service, this issue should not have a serious effect on our decision."

45 Error of Overconfidence

This error is another perceptual error and causes a person to be trapped in the path of wrong choices due to the belief that they are not capable.

Courtesy of Ryan McGuire

Courtesy of SHVETS production

46
The Error of Personalizing Issues

When making a decision, we should not see problems as circumstantial.

Courtesy of Gerd Altmann

47 Cognitive Conflict Error

This error occurs when there are conflicts between our mentalities and assumptions and our real life.

"We believe in fighting corruption, but in practice we pay bribes to do personal work."

Courtesy of Cottonbro

48
Neglecting the Positive Error

In an incident, we must see the positive and negative points to have a correct understanding of it.

49
Mind Reading Error

Most of us try to read what we like from other person's mind and make decisions based on that.

Courtesy of Olly

Courtesy of Ryan McGuire

Courtesy of Florin Radu

50
Unfair Comparison Error

A person interprets the surrounding events based on unrealistic standards.

51 False Confidence Effect Error

We reject all the evidence that contradicts our opinions and look for signs to validate our decision.

Courtesy of Andres Ayrton

52 The Musts Error

If we have defined unchangeable principles based on "must," our decisions fall under its influence.

53 Error of Projection

Seeing all people from our own point of view and compare their ability or lack of ability with us.

"Every mad man thinks all other men mad."

Courtesy of Alex Green

Courtesy of Gerd Altmann

54
Transposition Error

Is your recognition of a person in the first minutes of meeting them and after a while the same?

Courtesy of Tara Winstead

55

The Error of Intensifying the Obligation

When a person insists on implementing a wrong decision and continuing it in order to fulfill the obligation of a wrong decision.

Courtesy of Nadezhda Moryak

56 Error of Access

Our mind makes decisions based on available information, not based on facts.

57 Effect of Gentleness and Central Tendency Error

Gentleness is a personal characteristic that always evaluates others and events in a positive way. Gentle people usually refrain from describing others negatively and rate others highly and positively in all aspects, regardless of their actual performance.

The centrality tendency refers to this personal characteristic that a person avoids extreme judgment and evaluates all people and events as average or neutral, regardless of low or high performance.

58 Error of Conflict Theory

When we are more emotionally involved in a specific situation or issue, we show more tendency towards that phenomenon.

"When we are hungry, we should not go food shopping."

59 Error of Rarity Effect

If something becomes rare, it will severely affect our decisions, even if we do not need it.

Courtesy of Kate Trifo

Courtesy of Andrea Piacquadio

Courtesy of Karolina Grabowska

60

Additional Cost Error

When we have paid a lot for something, we don't dare to give it up, even though there is a possibility of losing more resources in the future.

61 Source Validation Error

The environment and the surrounding people can easily influence our decisions.

"Every human being is the average of five people close to them."

Courtesy of Cottonbro Studio

Mvezo Karamchand Hay

Courtesy of Oleksandr Pidvalnyi

62

Recency Error

Every new event or thing is not necessarily better than the previous one.

63

The Error of Not-Understanding The Mechanism

In general, our mind sees the final product and excludes its production and implementation process.

Courtesy of Skytoner

64
Gestalt Theory Error

According to this theory, the whole differs from the sum of its parts.

For instance, we cannot understand the experience of listening to the entire piece by listening to the individual notes of a symphony orchestra. The music produced by the orchestra is more than the sum of distinct notes played by various musicians. The song has a unique compositional quality that differs from the sum of its parts.
What we see is an object, its surroundings, and what we like to see.

Courtesy of Cottonbro Studio

Courtesy of Matt Jerome Connor

65
Black Swan Error

Ignoring impossible possibilities in calculations makes us forget about future events.

"Many people thought the swan was only white and did not see the possibility of the black swan until it happened."

Courtesy of Nattanan Kanchanaprat

66
Vector Error

In various fields, we expect that when a phenomenon grows, this vector will always be upward and smooth, so we remove this element that may suffer a drop and change from the decision making calculations.

"The best example of this error is the height and weight growth chart, which always grows during the early years of life."

67
The Error of Predicting the Future based on Past Events

Looking back in time to predict the future is the error of predicting the future based on past events.

"For instance, if a shepherd takes care of a flock of sheep by providing food, a place to sleep, and treatments, it means he will not butcher them one day."

Courtesy of Ekrulila

Courtesy of Coltombo Studio

68

Error of Evidence Denial

Where we deny the validity of the evidence that conflicts with our beliefs or desires, we can easily overlook or downplay the importance of contradictory evidence in favor of what we want to believe.

69
The Error of Making a Narrative

Expressing a linear event based on essential data.

We remember the details of today's breakfast, but we do not remember the clothes of the people we saw in the subway, so we tell stories to preserve this part.

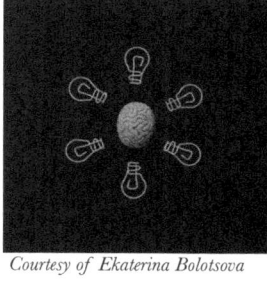

Courtesy of Ekaterina Bolotsova

Courtesy of Cottonbro Studio

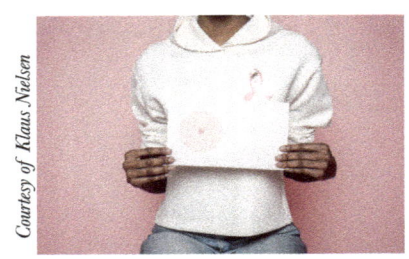
Courtesy of Klaus Nielsen

Courtesy of Nataliya Vaitkevich

70

Self-Care Error

We avoid doing some specific things for fear of the consequences which might happen in the future.

71
Error of the Threats

Failure to recognize all the factors that threaten us, causes us to make gross mistakes.

"The competitor of a cinema may not be a nearby cinema but a restaurant or a park. Or, the most critical threat to a casino may not be the professional gamblers; but the criminals who take the casino owner's child hostage."

Courtesy of Omar Houchaimi

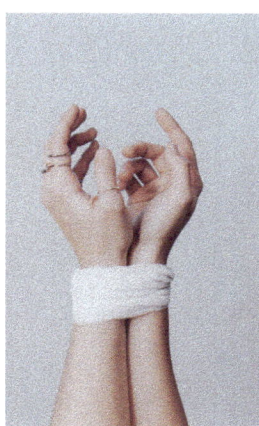
Courtesy of lil artsy

Courtesy of Tima Miroshnichenko

72
Error of Commitment Bias

It occurs when someone sticks with a course of action, even when presented with evidence to the contrary.

"The staff should only have a hot meal while perhaps calculating its value and paying in cash is more in the interest of the workers."

73

Scalable and Non-Scalable Information Misidentification Error

Our height and weight have physical limitations, so we have to deal with these numbers correctly. "We are not supposed to jump over a ten-meter object."

Courtesy of OpenClipart-Vectors

74 Information Deficiency Error

Focusing too much on what we know and neglecting what we don't know.

Courtesy of Mohamed Hassan

75 Limited Visibility Error

We must look at the problem from a different perspective to better understand a fact. "A person who looks at the train through a porthole sees only one wagon, while the bird sees the whole train."

76 Averaging Error

Another common mistake is relying on the averages that become the basis of a decision.

"Normally, the weather in winter in our city is not below zero, but on average, ten nights of a year, the temperature reaches 5 degrees below zero, so we should be mindful and prepare for ten nights."

Courtesy of Davyd Bortnik

77 Error of Negativity

From the news outlets' point of view, the bad news is good news, so the information that reaches us has more negative charge than the existing reality.

"Every day, we hear news about the death of children because of infectious disease, but we do not hear enough news about the children who survived because of the advancement of science."

78

Good Past Error

When nostalgia for past successes or events clouds the judgment of the current situation, this error is dangerous for decision-making. It can lead people to stick with outdated strategies and tactics that are no longer effective. This thinking can lead to complacency and stagnation rather than adaptation and innovation.

Courtesy of Cup of Couple

79

Fear and Size Error

We are often afraid of things that have nothing to do with us, and the size error can magnify it.
Take, for example, the fear of being bitten by a poisonous snake. We may look at the statistics of deaths caused by snake bites and spend every night worrying about dying this way when, in reality, it is an infrequent occurrence. These irrational fears can take over our lives if we do not take steps to challenge them.

Courtesy of MART Production

80 Massive Wrong Information Error

The negative mindset of people has made them believe that the world is constantly getting worse. This mistaken notion can lead us to feel discouraged and overwhelmed. As we become more aware of the positive aspects of our world, our minds will shift to a much more optimistic outlook.

Courtesy of Mohamed Hassan

81 Meaningless Numbers Error

It is easy to get lost in meaningless numbers if we fail to illuminate other factors in understanding the issue. "In the last twenty years, the United States has built no new dams; but Kenya makes a new dam every two years. Is the United States lagging behind Kenya? Is Kenya a leader in dam construction? The answer to this question is more complex, and we should consider that the U.S. has more stringent environmental regulations, which make dam construction more costly. Also, The American population is much more spread out than the Kenyan population, so the need for multiple dams is much less pressing."

Courtesy of Nina Garman

101 Cognitive Errors | 85

82 Immediate Decision Error

When we encounter a new situation, our first reaction is often to make a quick decision, resulting in a decision that may not be in one's best interests. How much of our decisions are based on an immediate event?

"War commanders make the best example of this type of decision-making. Which one of us is on the battlefield?"

George Chernilevsky

83 The Error of Fate

Fate plays a more prominent role in the end than our decisions.

"The doctor's mistake did not cause the patient's death, but his fate was to die like this."

Courtesy of Deagreez

84 Error of Generalizations

We can avoid making generalizations that do not accurately reflect the reality of the situation. "In general…" means not paying attention to the details of an event.

"In general, it does not rain in deserts."

Courtesy of Elianne

85 Blame Error

We often try to avoid making important decisions because of the fear that others will blame us for the outcome.

86

One-Dimensional Attitude Error

An error occurs when the individual relies solely on one viewpoint or opinion when making decisions, resulting in a biased outlook and disregarding other points of view. A person should take into consideration multiple sources of information, including current research and data, to make an informed and unbiased decision. Thinking critically and objectively is vital to make the best possible choice.

Courtesy of Josh Hild

87

Error of Fact in Practice

Knowing the theory of work is different from its implementation. Not being able to cook a good meal from a cookbook is the most obvious example of this error. We will never become good cooks by knowing the theory of cooking.

Courtesy of Malidate Van

88
Not paying Attention to the Limitations of Experts Error

Every person and specialist has the experience and expertise. One should not expect a doctor to become a great politician.

"As you sow, so shall you reap."

89 Cognitive Dissonance Error

When we find ourselves stuck between two conflicting opinions in our minds, it's challenging to make the right decision. This error happens when we convince ourselves that choosing the wrong path is correct. In such cases, we often find ourselves doing what is wrong, really good.

90
Contrast or Comparison Error

To reach a level that is defined for us, we make an unconventional decision.

"In order not to return the product in the store that has expired, we will auction that product."

91
Gamblers Error

When we have invested a lot in a project, and it is about to fail, we should get out of it as soon as possible.
Gamblers usually lose more and more under the pretext that there is still a chance of winning.

Courtesy of Josh Hild

92
Combination of Error

We often see the concept of law and justice through a limited perspective. When a law has addressed a specific issue, it is essential to evaluate whether this law will be effective in all situations. While effective in a limited area, some laws can become ineffective when they spread to a larger population. An example of this is a law that states that an individual who runs a red light will be fined; however, if everyone were to run the red light, would fining individuals still be the most effective solution?

93
Visual Change Error

Visual change does not equate to a deep understanding of the problem. Sometimes we decide what is desirable, but it is only an external change. The problem, however, remains the same. To illustrate this point, consider the question: By changing the steering wheel of a car from left to right, can it be claimed that the vehicle is suitable for driving in right-hand countries?

Courtesy of Intographics

94 Mental Belief Error

A common phenomenon wherein the human mind is prone to accepting information without question, regardless of its accuracy. This error is of believing something simply because most people believe in it provides a sense of comfort or pleasure.

Courtesy of Mohamed Hassan

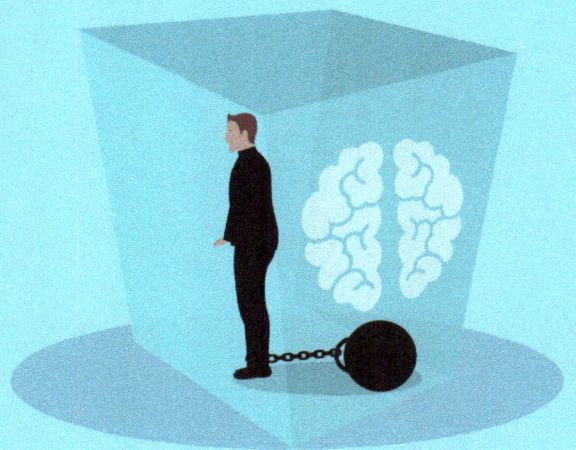

95 Founders' Trap Error

An inability to move away from the founders of the business. This error happens when a founder has an overbearing influence on the company and cannot cede control. Numerous challenges can arise in this situation, such as stagnation, lack of innovation, and difficulty scaling.

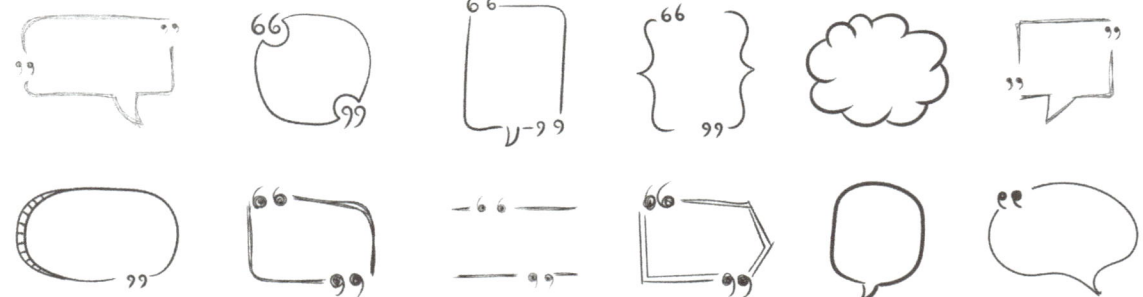

Courtesy of Little Monster 2070

96 The Error of Resorting to Preference

Courtesy of Gordon Johnson

Some believe that "quotes of the nobles" are a reliable way to make decisions and draw conclusions. Though a famous person may have expressed a profound opinion, it does not necessarily make a decision more valid.

97 Demanding Reasoning Error

To avoid being held accountable for a decision, we ask the opponents to give reasons for rejecting our decision.

Courtesy of SHVETS production

98
The Error of Appealing to the Majority

Any issue that the majority agrees or disagrees with is indeed correct.

Courtesy of Felipe Balduino

Courtesy of Zeeshaan Shabbir

99

The Cause and Effect Error

When an earlier event is seen as the underlying cause of a later event, but in reality, neither event was directly responsible for the other. This error can lead to flawed reasoning and misattributions of cause and effect.

"The accident resulted in the driver's death, although in some cases, the driver's pre-existing heart condition was the primary cause."

100 The Error of Analogy and Inference

A false assumption is inferred from two correct assumptions.
"When a drug is helpful for a patient's disease, we recommend it to others."

101 Magic Tricks Error

Illusion error is when our eyes cannot fabricate a reality of an image. This wrong impression of what's happening can easily lead to a wrong decision.
"An example of this is in car accidents; the driver may claim that they did not see the victim in time to prevent the collision."

—F×M—

www.ingramcontent.com/pod-product-compliance
Lightning Source LLC
Chambersburg PA
CBHW051332110526
44590CB00032B/4485